Every child counts. It is the
responsibility of every adult to
cherish and protect them.

Nothing. Else. Matters.

This book is dedicated to Chloe and Aubrey Berry,
and to their incredible mother Sarah. All profits
go to the Victoria Child Abuse Prevention and
Counselling Centre.

ISBN: 9798650706632

What does a Caterpillar do?

Written by David McArthur and illustrated by Lucy Rogers

Does a caterpillar
light our way at night?

No!

A firefly lights
our way at night

Does a caterpillar
catch flies in a web?

Does a caterpillar make
silk for our clothes?

No!

A silkworm makes
silk for our clothes

Does a caterpillar make
music with her feet?

No!

A cricket makes
music with her feet

Does a caterpillar have superhero strength?

No!

An ant has
superhero strength

Does a caterpillar carry her home on her back?

No!

A snail carries his home on his back

Does a caterpillar wear
a red and black coat?

No!

A ladybug wears a
red and black coat

Does a caterpillar have a hundred legs?

Does a caterpillar
make herself look
like a stick?

No!

A stick insect
makes himself look
like a stick

Does a caterpillar pollinate flowers in our garden?

No!

A bee pollinates
flowers in our garden

Does a caterpillar
glitter in the sun?

No!

A dragonfly
glitters in the sun

If a caterpillar doesn't wear a red and black coat, have a hundred legs, or glitter in the sun, then...

what does
she do?

She turns into a
beautiful butterfly!

For Chloe and Aubrey

Printed in Great Britain
by Amazon